Digging Up the Dead

ALSO BY MICHAEL KAMMEN

Visual Shock: A History of Art Controversies in American Culture

A Time to Every Purpose: The Four Seasons in American Culture

American Culture, American Tastes: Social Change and the 20th Century

Robert Gwathmey: The Life and Art of a Passionate Observer

In the Past Lane: Historical Perspectives on American Culture

Mystic Chords of Memory: The Transformation of Tradition in American Culture

A Machine That Would Go of Itself: The Constitution in American Culture

People of Paradox: An Inquiry concerning the Origins of American Civilization